This Time, Tomorrow

A Compendium of Laboured Voices from the Zambian 'Komboni'

Mwange Kauseni

Compiled and Edited by: Malama Katulwende

authorHOUSE®

AuthorHouse™ UK
1663 Liberty Drive
Bloomington, IN 47403 USA
www.authorhouse.co.uk
Phone: 0800.197.4150

Published by AuthorHouse 10/28/2016

ISBN: 978-1-5246-6471-8 (sc)
ISBN: 978-1-5246-6472-5 (e)

Print information available on the last page.

Any people depicted in stock imagery provided by Thinkstock are models, and such images are being used for illustrative purposes only.
Certain stock imagery © Thinkstock.

This book is printed on acid-free paper.

Because of the dynamic nature of the Internet, any web addresses or links contained in this book may have changed since publication and may no longer be valid. The views expressed in this work are solely those of the author and do not necessarily reflect the views of the publisher, and the publisher hereby disclaims any responsibility for them.

Contents

Foreword

I first made my acquaintance with Mwange Kauseni when I was thirteen. At that time, my parents had decided to send me to St Charles Lwanga Seminary School in Mansa to begin my journey as a Catholic priest, but also to acquire the superior education offered at an institution run by White Fathers. Mwange, on the other hand, was far ahead of me. As a Diocesan Brother, he had barely two years remaining of his seven years training as a Catholic priest, having studied philosophy, psychology, social anthropology, social communications, college English, social-political questions and the sacred scriptures at Mpima Major Seminary in Kabwe, and studied more theology and pastoral work at St Dominic's Major Seminary in Lusaka. When Mwange arrived in St Charles Lwanga, however, he came to serve as a teacher of civics and history. We learnt that the Rector at St Dominic's, obviously in consultation with the Bishop of Mansa and Mwange's Spiritual Father, had forced him on an indefinite probation for reasons which were not disclosed to anyone. It was assumed that during that probationary period, Mwange would teach and meditate on the sacred realities pertaining to his calling as a Catholic clergy.

Brother Max, as we fondly called him, settled down amongst his fellow staff, many of whom had come from far flung countries such as Canada, France, Ireland, England, France, Germany, and India, respectively. There were a few indigenous teachers, though. Our Rector was Fr Amyot d'Inville (who replaced Fr Stanger); and then we had Jean Tylee, Collin Scott, Anthony Slattery, Br Kalimba, Sr Estelle Clavette, Ambrose Kafindo, Tony Ben, Fr Stanslous Chibwe and a Mr. Tosh who taught us arithmetic. As compared to most public schools, St Charles Lwanga Seminary was indeed a small institution of about hundred and fifteen pupils, selected from some of the most rural and poor parishes of Luapula province of Zambia, yet famous country-wide for its excellent academic standing and morals. In those days, this Vatican-funded seminary school attracted pupils of very high intellectual calibre, who were rigorously selected at grade six by the seminary itself. It was, therefore, a very rare privilege to learn at such an institution, but more so to teach pupils whose minds and young souls were totally engaged in spiritual meditation and books.

As a adolescent boy, my first recollection of Brother Max at the time are that he was a slim, tall and lanky young man in his late twenties, with a long black, he-goat for a beard, full afro-hair and a hearty laugh. He was handsome, fair in complexion, and had a broad smile. Brother Max was a very social being, and I never saw him upset with anyone. He, like most of our teachers in St Charles Lwanga, mixed freely with seminarians. We played indoor games with him, especially basketball, and he sometimes ate with us in the dining hall. He particularly liked seminarians who read books and asked all kinds of questions - especially those of a political nature. I was in that category.

Looking back at those formative years of my life, I now see how I was inspired by Brother Max. He had studied theology and philosophy under some of the best professors and teachers of Catholic extraction, and he understood the polemics of philosophical thought and logical discourse. I was very young at the time, yet even then I sensed something peculiar in his eyes, facial expressions, and in his every word which fell from his lips. He was totally different from other staff. In class and outside class, Brother Max cut a figure of someone who was intrigued by the abstract. He was like a painter who, drawing from nature and experience to craft the intricacies and uplifting tendencies of art, nonetheless used his words to paint *that* reality – often hidden in figures of speech and extraordinary allegories. Brother Max applied language very watchfully, as he approached the same meaning by using synonyms. I understand this now, because I am a writer – this infinite desire to define objective reality but never quite arriving at the essence of the idea, this insatiable thirst for perfection. Like a true artist he kept painting, repainting and painting reality all over again, as if he was clutching at a realism which was always a fathom. Yet he had a deep sense of truth and social justice too, and it appeared to me that in the readings which he spoke to us about, he seemed a revolutionary.

Now I do not speak of revolutionaries in the sense of vandals, demagogues, the pretentious and vulgar who do not fully grasp the dialectics of social systems, but of revolutionaries and radicals in the Neo-Marxist and Afro-centric sense. He was a dialectician who sought fundamental societal change. In his life and works, Mwange always stood up for the poor, the downtrodden, the widow, the helpless, the marginalised and the persecuted. Brother Max had that avant-garde temper which set him apart from anyone religious I had come across. Intellectually very sharp, witty and always in command of the poetic imagery, he evoked in all of us the love for the written word, and an appreciation of the poetic life. We had very outstanding teachers, no doubt, yet Brother Max towered above them all for his great quality of mind, depth of sentiment, and deep sense of humanity.

I recollect that he read the African classics, from Chinua Achebe, Wole Soyinka, Leopold Senghor, Ngugi wa Thiongo, Sol T Plaatje, to Steve Bantu Biko of South Africa. Here at home, he often quoted Simon Mwansa Kapwepwe, Stephen Mpashi and Dr. Kenneth Kaunda with great zest. When he read Kapwepwe's work, *"Afrika Kuti Twabelela Uluse Lelo Tekuti Tulabe"*, for example, his voice sounded as though he had recited a canticle. No one could ever forget the spontaneous creation and performance of poetry in class, nor the imagery of those fantastic books he had read in English, Bemba, Greek or Latin. I was too young to comprehend the classics, but through him I "read" great authors whose works I was to meet a little later in life, when at the age of sixteen, I started to write literary reviews. Brother Max spoke about books without exerting any mental effort, and I was amazed at the depth of his knowledge and appreciation of the literary landscape. As it turned out, though, Brother Max only spent a short time a St Charles Lwanga Seminary. By that time I had gone to a different seminary school; namely, Lubushi Seminary, where I discovered myself as a writer and decided to pursue that literary path. I declined the priestly calling in Mpima Major Seminary and instead attended the University of Zambia.

During these turbulent years of my life as an undergraduate, I had lost contact with Brother Max. Yet I heard of him and always kept him in my mind. I carved out a literary life and, as chance would have it, first published my poetry in an anthology titled *Under the African Skies: Poetry from Zambia* in 2003. Two years later, I made my first break as an international writer with my novel, *Bitterness*, published in the United States of America. The following year, I won the Julius Chongo Award for the Best Creative Writer in Zambia at the Ngoma Awards Ceremony. At that time, I had decided to settle in the capital city, Lusaka, and start out as an entrepreneur and pursue my literary career in my spare time. It was then that I learnt where Brother Max was: he had just started working for PANOS Africa. After tracking where his office was, I met up with my former teacher whom I had last seen nearly two decades ago. We hugged – it was a tearful moment for me, I should confess - and Mwange told me that firstly, he had never forgotten me, but had always believed that I was an intellectual rebel who was as sharp as a Jesuit.

He confided that despite writing a number of poems over the years, he had not quite made up his mind to publish anything yet. As a perfectionist myself, I knew what he meant. We spoke about publishing prospects in Zambia, and I advised that he tries abroad considering the fact that poetry as a genre was very difficult to place for publication. At this point, Mwange suggested that I find time to look at his work and give him an opinion. I accepted, but little did I know that this was the last time I was destined to see him ever again. We were both very busy in our own worlds, and the circumstances of our lives made it impossible for us to meet. He travelled a lot, and the pressure of my business enterprise drew much of my attention. I did not know that he had died in October 2006, however, until three years later when I met his younger brother Mwaba, and much later a Catholic friar named Brother Mike Safeli, who had lived with Mwange and witnessed the last moments of his life.

It is always incredible how certain individuals come into this world, rub shoulders with you, and leave impressions destined to last a lifetime. Such was Brother Max. His unconventional character was such that it made him stand out from the crowd and appear larger than life. When I conferred with Brother Mike Safeli at the Franciscan House in Emmasdale, Lusaka, we laughed heartedly at some eccentricities which Mwange exuded. Single-minded and tenacious in those beliefs which he held dear, Mwange lived poetry and never lost sight of this vocation. It was the most important calling in his life, and he had no shadow of doubt in his mind that one day he would see the fruits of his labours in print. Regrettably, however, this was not to be.

In April of this year (2016) the family of the late poet finally resolved to publish his works under the title, *This Time Tomorrow* in honour of Mwange's wishes and his memory. Since no one had any experience with the process of editing and preparing a book for publication, the family approached Dr. Buleti Nsemukila, a demographer, statistician and lecturer at the University of Zambia. Dr. Nsemukila begged to be excused and suggested that he could only think of one person who might be best suited to do the job – Malama Katulwende. The scientist gave me a call and insisted that I take up the task to compile, edit, and prepare Mwange's work for publication. I did not refuse the responsibility. As a matter of fact, Dr. Nsemukila and I come from Lubwe; we both attended the same schools - St Charles Lwanga, Lubushi Seminary School and the University of Zambia, respectively. As seminarians, we battled each other on the tennis court and ping pong. And for all these years he has been a brother and mentor to me.

I set up an appointment to meet Mwange's widow, Katemba, and indeed we discussed the details of the project in my office the following Saturday. She explained the situation, and recollected that Mwange had spoken to her about me and editing his works. As she narrated this, I felt extremely humbled. I vowed that I would do whatever it took to get this book into print. The work had literary merit and deserved to be brought out into the public domain. I also wanted to do this task in honour of my teacher, friend and elder brother, who lit a literary path for me.

Katemba gave me the flash drive on which Mwange Kauseni's work, *This Time, Tomorrow,* was saved. I recollect that in our conversations, Mwange had alluded to some of the poems I was now able to read, and I was astonished at their freshness and impact they exerted on me. *This Time Tomorrow* stretches two decades of creative writing. In compiling the collection, I have examined and picked only those poems which were thematically diverse and stylistically different to be part of the anthology. I have tried as much as possible to preserve Mwange's identity as an artist, recognising that the works in question were an embodiment of a man who was very perceptive of his circumstances and comprehended his place in the wider scheme of things. The reader will observe, however, that some of the poems have been overtaken by historical time. They read a little obsolete.

In order to fully appreciate the material circumstances which shaped these poems, it is important to view the work in an historical context. Zambia gained independence from Britain in 1964. From that time up to Mwange's death in 2006, the post-colonial Zambia had passed through two distinct political phases. From 1964 to 1991, the country was under the tutelage of the United National Independence Party (UNIP), led by Dr. Kenneth Kaunda. Under his leadership, Dr. Kaunda introduced socialism and a one-party state, whereby the major business assets in mining, manufacturing, retailing, construction, transport, telecommunications and postal services, were nationalised and wholly owned by the state. Dr. Kaunda also introduced an African political philosophy called humanism, which guided the investment climate and political economy of the country. Under the 27 years of UNIP rule, the landlocked nation scored some successes but also went through political repression and economic stagnation. Towards the end of the 1980s, Zambia had reached a tipping point. Prices of metals and other commodities on the international markets had plunged, whereas the oil price shot up. For Zambia, which was heavily dependent on copper earnings for its foreign exchange, this scenario meant that the country's reserves shrunk, as oil imports surged upwards. The government, which owned a majority stake in the mining industry under ZCCM, had problems reinvesting in new production technology and keeping operation costs down. Under the circumstances, it was only a matter of time before the mining industry ground to a halt. There was a popular uprising against the high cost of living, political intolerance, and the scarcity of basic goods and services in the copper-rich nation. The UNIP-led regime lost much of its popular appeal from the masses. Two years later, Dr. Kaunda lost an election to a trade unionist named Frederick Chiluba, who introduced multiparty politics and capitalism.

With this change in political economy came the IMF and World Bank programs. To access concessionary loans from these international lenders, the Chiluba's MMD regime was compelled to plug the leaks into those sectors which haemorrhaged public funds. Therefore, to bring the cost of running the public sector down, the new government embraced the IMF-World Bank austerity measures, by down-sizing its civil service, and privatising major state assets such as mines, insurance, manufacturing, agricultural ranches, and railway and road transport businesses. As a consequence of these radical reforms, thousands of people lost their jobs and livelihoods. Social insecurity and discontent started to rise. The economy was in such a dire state that poverty, unemployment, labour migration, and disillusionment defined everything. The populism and political rhetoric of Chiluba and his promises of a prosperous Zambia were fading fast. There were no considerable direct foreign investments into the country. By 2006, therefore, most Zambians had grown somnolent of the Chiluba-led reforms as they only seemed to guarantee and reinforce social inequalities and the prevailing levels of extreme poverty in the country. Unless something fostered this trend, there was a likelihood of social strife. Every day, Zambia lost some of its needed human resource such as teachers, lectures, engineers, medical doctors and nurses. They fled to Europe, America, Australia, New Zealand and other prosperous African countries such as South Africa, Botswana, Namibia, Swaziland, Lesotho, and Kenya for economic opportunities.

Intellectually, the landscape was equally a reflection of this state of social, political and economic decay. The publishing industry was almost on its knees; several companies such as Printpak, Zambia Printing Company, and Kenneth Kaunda Foundation - which later became Zambia Education Publishing House (ZEPH) - were either folding their presses or were insolvent. The production of artistic books by the state-owned Zambia Education Publishing House (ZEPH) was reduced to a few works per year. The music industry was also almost non-existent. Television and radio productions, too, were in a state of deterioration or decline. In terms of intellectual output, this period will be defined as a watershed in Zambia's history. There was very little, or nothing of consequence produced. The greater focus of most Zambians appeared to be their preoccupation with the economy and the political cynicism prevailing in the country. Although it was anticipated that with the re-introduction of politics, democracy and the free flow of ideas would flourish, the political atmosphere was characterised by instances of repression and certain forms of dictatorship which were reminiscent of the past. For example, the selective application of the Public Order Act and the lacunas in the justice system, justified the suspicion that the government dealt unlawfully with its perceived opponents. Just as it was in the Kaunda era, so were voices of dissent silenced with violence, threats, police harassment and brutality and imprisonment by the ruling class. Political space became ever more contested between the ruling class who wanted to keep the status quo, on the one hand, and opposition political parties, NGOs, the Church and private media such as the Post newspaper, on the other hand, who advocated for change.

Speaking of the international geopolitical situation, the period between 1990 and 2006 saw the collapse of the Berlin Wall, the Unification of Germany, the end of the Cold War, the demise of the USSR, the end of Apartheid, and African civil wars in Sudan, Angola, Mozambique, Somalia, Eritrea and Ethiopia, and much of West Africa. African voices who brandished Pan Africanist ideologies were dying out one by one. Thus the philosophies of Humanism, Negritude, Ujamaah and other African-bred ideological perspectives against colonialism and imperialism, were all struggling to remain relevant to the problems and challenges of the contemporary world. The imperialists and colonialists had left, yet Africa still remained a citadel of civil wars, hunger, disease, poverty and underdevelopment. The question which deserved an answer was – to what extent were Africans themselves to blame for their own underdevelopment?

To place the answer in perspective, let us recollect that post-colonial Africa produced a fundamental shift in intellectual environment in which most writers on the continent began to question the role of African elites and the ruling class in the under-development of Africa. This started with Chinua Achebe, Ngugi wa Thiong'o, Wole Soyinka and Ayi Kwei Ahmah, to cite some examples, who waged a battle against the new political leaders. Unfortunately, not only did these African "elites" become self imposed dictators and violators of human rights, they also looted public funds and stashed them into foreign bank accounts. The new ruling class connived with foreign agents to appropriate resources outside their countries, thus becoming agents of neo-colonialism. What were writers and artists on the continent supposed to do? Well, these creative minds redefined their roles as artists and began to use art as a means of social and political change. Utilising the power of their pens, the writers clashed with imperialism and neo-colonialism in general and criticised a small clique of their own people - the new ruling class – for transforming their own countries into failed states. This struggle is quite evident in Mwange's work.

It is also important to state that Mwange also drew much inspiration from the circumstances of his life as an author and journalist. After graduating from the Africa Literature Centre (ALC) in Kitwe in 1989 with distinction, Mwange launched his new career as a journalist by working for a year at the Diocese of Mansa as communications coordinator. He then moved on, in 1992, to work for the Daily Mail and Sunday Mail, respectively, in Lusaka, as a sub-editor. The following year he decided to work abroad – in Botswana, where he lived for more than a decade. Thus Mwange worked at Pen-Point Enterprises (Pty) in Gaborone, as a managing editor and principal consultant from 2000 to 2003. He was a news editor at Botswana's leading newspaper, Mmegi The Reporter. Mwange also worked as sub-editor at the Botswana Guardian/Midweek Sun Group of Newspapers, and the Business Focus Magazine. In 2004 he returned back to his home country, Zambia, and worked as an independent consultant. His areas of specialisation as a journalist were training trainers, public relations, feature writing, investigative reporting as well as negotiations and editing skills training. Mwange also wrote for regional and international publications including The Sunday Times of South Africa, The Post (Zambia), and the Africa News Bulletin (ANB), Brussels, Belgium.

As a journalist, therefore, Mwange Kauseni was privileged to travel across the globe for work. He travelled to Rupohlding, Germany, where he received the Journalist of the Year Award in 1989; Sao Paulo, Brazil; Dakar, Senegal; Johannesburg, South Africa; and as an independent consultant alongside twenty three other international journalists, he monitored and evaluated the hand-back of Hong Kong to Mainland China by Britain in 1996. His experiences in these places are reflected in some of his poems such as *Rainbow Brazil*, *I Miss My Country* and *Post Card To Hong Kong*.

Furthermore, Mwange drew from his life as a Catholic faithful, and an ex-seminarian who was so profoundly religious as to attempt to become a priest. Having spent nearly seven years in the Mpima and St Dominic's seminaries, respectively, he was fully aware of the Catholic Social Teaching, the papal encyclicals and the duties of every Catholic towards the poor. In almost his works, this pro-poor attitude is very clearly evident. His poems always echo the cries and despair of the marginalised and the helpless, and he battles against the political establishment who are opposed to the expectations of the masses. Further, his work demonstrates his experiences of exile, bond with his country and culture, and the love for Africa. His life – which transcended his own person - represents a new Africa, a new renaissance. For this very reason, it is my sincere hope that these poems will be appreciated for their pan Africanist character on the African continent. It is also hoped that this work will offer hope and inspiration to everyone who will come into contact with it.

In compiling, editing and preparing this work for publication, I closely worked with several members of the late poet's family without whom it would not have been possible to complete this task. I am, therefore, indebted to Mwaba Kauseni, Mwange's brother, for many insights into the poet's life. I am also thankful to Katemba, Mwange's widow, and their children, for their support in providing the original manuscript, family photographs, and narratives of the poet's life. Finally I am grateful to Mwange's friends – especially Brother Mike Safeli for their valuable support and encouragement in making Mwange's dream come true. This is what Mwange would have liked to happen. It is my privilege to have contributed a small part in this.

Born on the 2nd July 1960, Mwange Kauseni really wanted to become a Catholic priest but abandoned his vocation in 1985 out of frustration over his prolonged probation. He is survived by his wife, Katemba and three children.

Malama Katulwende
Lusaka, October 2016

Prologue

To all my friends and one-time students:
May you, by standing on my shoulders,
see far beyond
what I myself have seen.

May the heights of the mountains
never scare you
nor the intensity of the darkness
ever intimidate you.

Come what may
never say die:
Amala ya mwaume
yashala kucishiki!

Preface

Yesterday was
scornfully bad
Today scandalously worse

If nothing changes
soon

If we remain in the gutter still
while the elite continue
to get mid-term gratuity
and feast on our behalf

This time tomorrow
heads must roll

for how can a man wear a shirt
or a woman her *citenge*
in the day
and later use it as a blanket
for their child at night?

Or indeed
unpaid retirees die of shame and sorrow
all because
their pride as human beings
is gone on account of poverty
and they can't squarely face tomorrow!
No, *bane tefyo iya!!*

Dedication

To **HER** and to **ALL** -
without whom no book
could have been written.

Those that in failure stood in silence
by my side -
and in success sat in front
cheering the most.

Those that made *the* difference:
mom and dad, brothers and sisters
all-weather friends (they know themselves)
and indeed beloved wife, Katemba
and angelic children Bupe-Kunda
Bwalya and Mwange

May the rainbow of love
illuminate your personal skies and ever keep at bay
the undesirable storms that make this
otherwise wonderful life so blue.

Loving you always - this work is FOR you guys
for making my life worth its while
in spite of all the turmoil.

Day by day you confidently talked of my star rising once again
and of God in his own time
confounding and scattering my enemies in all directions
as He announces a New Dawn for me.

Your word has come to pass, may God bless you for it all,
Muli bantu!

Child of Fate at Kasisi

I first saw you in an orphanage,
Kasisi,
and have ever since carried you
in my heart.
As we sat in the chapel
singing glory to God in the highest
I prayed for peace here on earth below
for you
knowing with no real mother or father
you are a child of the earth and the universe,
a child of fate.

Wherever I go
you repeatedly catch my mind's attention;
you deserve some mention.
Your teary eyes tell long tales of
painful meditations
as your mouth silently sings about
suppressed longings known to none.
Your bloated feet nurse invisible blisters
sustained from endless travels along
hidden paths of a troubled mind -
You deserve sympathy
I bestow empathy.

When exhausted and desperate
your burdened head rests upon the bosom
of a mother you have never seen
and in innocent fright
your broken heart yearns for
the understanding heart of a father

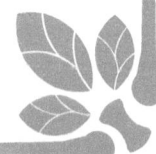

1

you have never known -
You yearn for solidarity
I pledge fraternity.

In my numerous travels
I have met your brother too -
tiny, naked, dead
aborted and thrown onto a rubbish heap,
his only clothing:
a polyethylene bag.
Looking into his decomposed eyes
my own eyes burst into a torrent of tears.
His distorted toothless mouth refused to sing
even a sad song for a world too impersonal,
I agreed with him,
and as his motionless feet hastened
to the world of the immortal
I bade him a sad farewell
and told him with a sob,
I, too, am a Child of Fate
waging my own unending battles
every minute
every day.

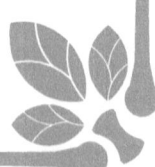

Letter to Chibale-Kalaba

Chibale-Kalaba, listen:
I lately met the late Mambwe,
'The African Savage' Mulenga
and he sent no greetings to anyone;
he still is a bitter man
over the cultural barrenness that has
perpetually smitten our land.

Greg Lungu also wondered
if the path he began to beat
through 'Play Circle'
was now finished;
And all I could defensively mutter was:
My brother, how could I know
when I now reside in Botswana
confounded by the beauty of its local song and dance.
Ba wesu, you just have to see the *Tswana*
egalitarian version of doing things!

Patu Simoko
was as witty as ever and
posed his old prickly question:
Why underdevelopment?
To him I explained how
we now have a matrix of sorts at play
in which the country moves in all directions
except forward as it awaits instructions
from the IMF and World Bank.
They talk about HIPC, I told him
with tears of anger in my eyes;
and he said in his time

3

the only bank that mattered after the Bank of Zambia
was Barclays.

Chibale, my brother,
our cultural waters these days
literally drip through our emaciated fingers
liberally - it nauseates!
Can't we flip through the old diaries of
Hagai Chisulo
Matsautso Phiri
Stephen Chifunyise
Maurice Tembo
Dickson Mwansa
Darius Lungu
Mumba Kapumpa and
Ba Mudala ba Joseph Kabwe
for some fresh inspiration?

Where is
Matilda Malama-Mfumu, by the way?
Jane Lungu
Kalasa Kuseka and
Joseph Kawesha,
any *info* about them?
And now I hear
there is Mulenga Kapwepwe
nabena Pontiano Kaiche.

I hear Anthony Kunda
ran out of revolutionary ink
and chose the path of silence
while Bright Mwape migrated
with all his brightness
out of frustration to Namibia.

Thank Sausande,
Ben Phiri
Kapotwe and Maximo
for providing the people with laughter
in these caustic times of artistic disaster.

And ask the so-called Minister of Culture,
if ever there is one,
to give enough kwacha
to the cause of preserving
Insaka yesu Fwebena Afrika
without which
we are not a people!

After this, I am writing
to *Bashi* Mpundu Kapwepwe
and *Ba* Bwembya Mushindo
informing them that I have written to you
about these very impassioned matters.
I wonder if our very own Shakespeare,
Ba Mpashi, is still around
and it would be interesting to know
if Hector Kaonga is also there.
One hell of an actor that you must prod into
some real action, if you can.

Write back soon
and talk about Nataaz
and its unending razzmatazz.
Any silver lining on the horizon?

Tell Nkandu Kapepula
his silence isn't golden at all
and ask him where I can find
our erstwhile drama guru

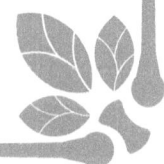

Maurice Chishimba of the *Kanchule*
Na Lona fame.

I hear publishing is still a big hassle at home,
and I cry, thinking about rotting mountains of
explosive manuscripts
like your masterpiece: *I returned to my country*!

My regards to all newcomers to the struggle:
Urge them to be united, resilient and strong,
otherwise, like we have counselled now and again
They won't last!

If our gods keep us well,
as they have always done,
Chibale, we shall meet soon
and once again *Celebrate Our Awareness*.

Greetings to Mutale Bowa.
What became of his popular programme,
Poets' Corner?

Post Script:
[*This poem was initially written in 1995 when Chibale, a great artist friend of mine, was still alive - and we had chance to briefly discuss it. It is for that very sentimental reason that I do not want to over-edit it. I later learnt with great grief, of Chibale's demise - long after his death, all because I was away in Botswana for a considerably long time. I also later learnt that a host of other colleagues, including Anthony Kunda, Bright Mwape, Nkandu Kapepula, Joseph Kawesha, Maximo, Sauzande and many more are no more. My heart bleeds for them all. May the great souls of these remarkable artists rest in eternal peace*].

Rainbow Brazil

In the golden arms of
Gorgeous Afro-Brazilian Graca
(Campos do Jordao)
I romantically lay
And she also in my black ones
Our new-found romance inspired by invisible
Ties of long-lost kinship
Via the heinous road-map of
Slave trade and destructive colonialism.

Quietly, tearfully,
Endearingly I heard her implore:
Can't I go back home
to Africa with you?
A question I painfully ignored
but silently explored: What is home
if all there is
is gun fire upon mortar fire
and endless ugly feasts by insatiable vultures
either side of the equator
on abundant human flesh
butchered with the aid of AK47s
and left to decompose
at liberty on desert sand
with the last homage paid only by
helpless cactus trees.
What indeed is home
when all the people know
is birth and death
with nothing in between!
What indeed is home

when a whole starving continent
relies on the teaspoon of the West
to grudgingly dole out donor food
as brother watches brother and sister
collapse and die
on an endless queue!
Is a sentimental return to the African continent,
worth any trouble,
after centuries upon centuries of
marriages and intermarriages
that have now produced
a multicoloured Brazil
such a poetic rainbow population?

I nudged her to sleep
cuddled in my protective embrace
humming some African lullaby
into her yearning ears
although later in my dreams
a land mine stupidly exploded
in Maputo
and another one in Luanda
to my terrible annoyance.

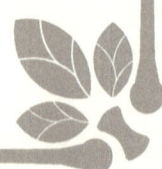

Harvest Time

After our own winter of discontent
hooray, it's harvest time.
May the farmer enjoy
the fruit of his labour.
Watch the migrant bird gracefully return
from winter's leave
to festivity.

The pigeon of hope
clutching in its beak an olive branch
announces its return, adding colour
and elegance to the garden of life.
Face beaming with a hopeful smile
in readiness to preach
the gospel of recreation
equity and fair play
the god of retribution announces
the break of a new dawn.

The swallow and sparrow are back
and the ominous black cat has gone
into hibernation to remind us all - there is indeed
a time for everything.

The more reason why
it must be your turn
my pot-bellied brother
grown plump
like a hippo on tax payers' money
to quietly, gracefully, voluntarily move aside
after reading the writing on the wall

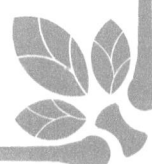

that the people won't deal with any dealer any more
Old or New -
this harvest season of equity and fair play.
Then,
umunoobe nga akubeepa ukukwiita
nobe umubeepe ukumwaasuka!!
Simple.
(If a fellow pretends to invite you,
you also pretend to answer back!).

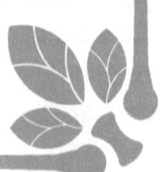

African Poets

Refuse to be bought
with chicken noodles, champagne
or indeed any khaki envelope;
make recourse to your conscience
and fight the rot
in the name of the people.
Aren't you Africa's modern prophets
charged with the task to prod those
that bask in indolence
to wake up and live?
Fold thy shirt sleeves and fight
those that in the name of politics
volunteer to lead a better life
on behalf of the people.
Yours is the duty
to restore dignity
to a people oppressed by their own
deviant sons and daughters
whose skin pigmentation or
cultural orientation is no longer certain.
In the natural arena
aren't you the water lilies upon whose fragile leaves
should rest
God's little birds of fortune
on their way to regain a lost paradise?
Or in the national arena
informal leaders
that must ensure the balance of the national equation?
In the construction industry
mustn't you be the bridge builders
that serve as bridges as well?

You just ought to be
part of the solution in a rickety world
facing dissolution.
Resist retrogression in the name of patriotism
and pursue a path of resoluteness
against the apparent maze of modernity.
Warriors of the pen,
align your energies with those
of Shaka, the great King of the Zulu.

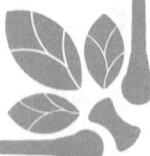

We Men and Women

The games we play
the traps we lay
the loves we fake
the hearts we break
the lies we lie

The tricks we employ
the masks we wear
the gimmicks we apply

The yeses we withhold
the nos we later regret

The romantic headaches we cause
for no apparent cause

So unfair
how we fair
We men
and women
sometimes so mean
nobody understands
just what we mean!

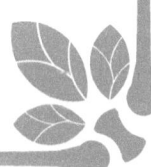

Lost Focus

Reminiscing on the fruitlessness
of yet another gone-by day
insomnia floods the minds and eyes
of Africa's younger generation
who today witness continental history repeat itself silly
on a daily basis.

Mesmerised, they watch
as one-time political luminaries
disappear from the African stage
into the gloomy valley of
no longer existent philosophies:
Mze Kenyatta's Harambee
Mwalimu Nyerere's Ujaama and
Comrade Kaunda's Humanism
among which somewhat survives
only a semblance of Senghor's Negritude
in adulterated Rasta poetry!

A *coup de tat* has taken place
and not only has the king been deposed
the throne has been desecrated,
the vision stolen
the arsenal dismantled!

And the political binoculars shows
there's no focus both
below and above the Equator.

A new debate has nevertheless been ignited
by patriotic younger warriors who,

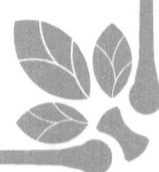

"no longer at ease" with the current crop of
political *mulattos,* curse in fury the
bastard sons and daughters
of the struggle who, now adorned in Western attire
and speaking with borrowed accents,
have hijacked the people's struggle
and taken the reins of power
only to masturbate on sacred shrines and kingdoms
upon which they are now constructing
with cardboard, chewing gum
sawdust and paper clips
subtle familydoms, clandoms
and cliquedoms they contend
are solid platforms and foundations
for Africa's redemption
while filling their already bloated stomachs
with the people's milk and honey
and locking away in their personal safes
the people's basic freedoms and rights!

"Ukuceenjela kumo, cimo nokutuumpa!"
(Some cleverness is worse than foolishness.)

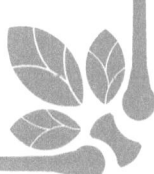

Fires of Commemoration

Chant
sons and daughters of Afrika
a proper requiem
to oil the bones of those
whose blood watered the original seeds of
our continental liberation.

Plant a new seed!

Gather pyres
and light fires of commemoration
for unsung heroes and heroines
of this flamboyant land.

Drive away evil spirits
with waters of personal purification
let all of us lead a life
worth emulation.

Let our land know peace like before!

Dust thy faces with ashes
and compose a song of repentance
while seeking the canonisation of
the Shakas and Kabakas
of the forgotten times.

Beat the *bongo* with pride
blast the *mwimbi* with dignity
tear the skies apart with incantation
sing a song of rededication

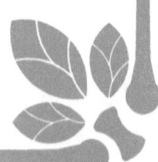

and revisit *Bashi Mwalule*
for fresh inspiration. The Hour has come!!

And the West is choking
with laughter

If we must effectively hide
anything from the African, they whisper and conspire,
hide it in a book for he that inhabits
the great continent of Africa
has no hunger
no passion or yearning for reading

Hide everything we value in a book
and once that is done
overdose the African
with trivia
and confuse him with our new-found
arbitrary vocabulary of
liberalisation
structural adjustment
HIPC and all that is hand-in-glove
with our new brand of colonialism -
Globalisation!

Meanwhile, Africa can't even properly spell
her own name AFRIKA
and the West is choking with
arrogant laughter!

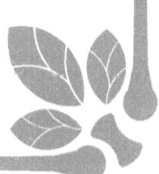

Write to right!

If the pen doesn't write
to right the wrongs and soothe the pain
of the nation -
If Pressmen
and women
let themselves be pressed
and kneaded like dough
into all sorts of ugly shapes -
If men of honour abuse their power
at will
and we all just sit and watch
and applaud,
where lies the nobility of the profession of the scribe?
Where lies a people's salvation
from constitutional vultures?
Indeed
if the city degenerates into a jungle of lawlessness
and the lowly and weak find no respite
even from the scribe
isn't this a crime, a shame?
When the **** hits the fan[1]
the pen must ejaculate a hybrid germ
that must put an end to the rotten trend
and in turn give birth
to a breed of warriors
deficient only in fear.

---

[1] I couldnt make out what Mwange meant here

I remember you

I recall with hidden pleasure
memories dearly preserved
in the deep-freezer of my adolescence
remembering the path
that stealthily took us to the village thicket
where, arm around waist
with a childish giggle
nipple to nipple
in village style
on bare ground
I got initiated
into the sweet-sour pleasures of adulthood
and lost without much protestation
my treasured childhood shyness and innocence.
Sweat odour tickled my nostrils
as in blissful ecstasy you systematically sobbed
in traditional style and cried for your mother repeatedly!

I still recall the colourful beads adorning your waist,
the kinky braids on your head -
and the black lustre that mesmerised me then
still remains a vivid beacon on the highway
of my masculinity.

And if to everyone's romantic history
there is a point of return
mine manifested itself at the beckoning fort of
your gorgeous coffee thighs
under the blazing African sun
to the accompaniment of

constant chirping and bleating of
small birds and African crickets under a *Mupapa* tree.

I swear
there will always be for you
a big thank you in my heart
and a possible repeat performance
if ever we meet again,
only this time, my dear,
with a *protection*
for the times have changed!

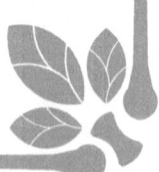

Woman of my Life

Of all that I know
love and adore
You gracefully stand out
huge and tall
dwarfing the rest of them all
in the jungle of my life
where you are
the solitary Baobab.

This song is for you
citadel of my being
Your milk still flows in my veins
and my life is an intractable fibre of praise
of your nobility

May tranquillity be your lot
as I, with the pen of my tongue
generously smear on the brow of your beautiful face
our traditional regal powder, *Inkula*.

Mother,
let me proudly hang around your graceful neck
the sum total of my being
for you are
The woman of my full and broken life.
And tomorrow
when I go to the river
that selflessly, like you, pours its simple waters
into the ocean, I will sit on its bank
as I used to cuddle on your lap,
and proclaim over and over again,
that you truly are
the WOMAN OF MY LIFE!

Where have all the flowers gone?

At dusk everyday
all the poor Zambian Curator does is enter
yet another lost chapter
in the history books of a one-time great nation.

And from yonder
comes an anguished voice of inquiry:

Where are the hippos
of the Kariba shores,
the impalas of the Luangwa Valley?

The gazelles of Mfuwe
and the Kasaba Bay tiger fish,
where are they?

Famous mines Nkana,
Chibuluma,
Nchanga and Konkola -
how did they become
peptic ulcers in the bowels of the nation?

Why does the tall Kalambo Falls
no longer fall but only trickles
while the ancient Mosi-o-tunya
no longer thunders
but just whimpers.

Zambia -
looking down at you from
the top of the Mchinga escarpment

yesterday
all I saw were holes in the pots
and potholes in the economy

And looking up at you today
from the Luapula Valley
all I see are holes in your knickers, blisters on your feet
and tears in the eyes of the people:

Where have all the flowers gone???

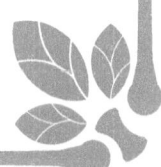

I miss my country

Aboard Airline Varig
Way above the Atlantic Ocean
I envision my country, Ng'umbo:
Mwankole Kumushi Kwamutende?

I am elated
Being homeward bound
From Rio to Ng'umbo
Yearning for the fresh waters of
Islands Chishi
Mbabala and the mainland.

There, where I have been,
There are too many bitches
On the sleazy beaches
Of Rio
And the dangerous streets
Of Sao Paolo.

I truly miss the pebbles and snail shells
On the virgin shores of
Lakes Bangweulu, Chifunabuli
And Kampolombo,
The simplicity and sanguine generosity
Of a people
Unspoilt by civilisation.
As I return
With nimble journalism on my tongue,
My country Ng'umbo
I won't cover your nakedness
There won't be any need for bashfulness
I will adorn it with abundant praise
As we dance *akalela* before we go to pray!

24

My better half

A stone cast into a pond
causes concentric circles

Your presence in my life
casts its own ripples around me
I feel splendidly engrossed
like an embryo
into the amniotic comfort of your being

My guardian angel,
away from you
I am a detached leaf
floating aimlessly hither and thither
wrapped into the wanton wings
of undirected winds

Your life and mine lie so entwined
without your presence
I am dead
really dead
haunted by my own ghost,
'rescuable'
only by YOU.

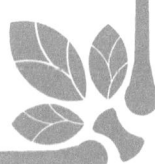

A family's lament

While dark clouds
crowd the skies
mother and child remain awake
short of a blanket, as usual

The child
forced into adulthood by poverty says:
Mother, with no roof over our hut
I feel afraid!

Shivering,
the mother manages a sob:
Son, a worse storm rends my heart
invisible tears flood my eyes
I am equally afraid.

The two cuddle against each other
as heaven and earth find intersection
through the unity of the rain,
mosquitoes chanting the accompanying tune,
their companions
rats and cockroaches.

It's getting too wet, mum
hold me closer, you are warmer

Nudging closer, forcing mucus back into her nostrils
she holds his cold hand and looks at his face

But the warmth the son feels
is only a mother's warmth

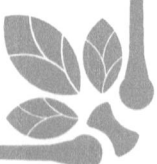

deep inside
she is so cold she could sit before ice
for warmth.

And lightning takes a picture of the duo,
each finding reason to live on
only for the other's sake.

But mother, why should it be only us
he enquires?

Wiping a tear with the back of her hand
she sobs and explains:
No my son
there are plenty others;
we are a clan and victims of fate,
the cast-aways whose bones creak as they walk

Can't someone organise
a protest match to parliament
or at least sing a loud song
at some freedom square
to show that this nonsense is wrong??

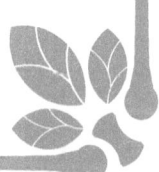

Ken Saro Wiwa

Without meeting
we met in thought and personal resolve
to call a spade a spade
We conversed in private meditation
distance notwithstanding -
drinking from the same well of inspiration

And armed with purity of intention
you sought for your people
dignity and equity
a language the military don't understand!

Wiwa - I shed a tear in memory of you
rest assured
the struggle will go on
beyond Ogoniland
to prove to the Son of Abacha
and those of his ilk
that for every Wiwa that gets murdered
a thousand more are born
to champion the cause of justice
there, here and beyond.
Aluta Continua!

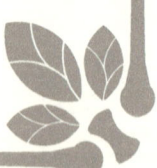

Post Card to Hong Kong

I still hear the sharp Cantonese greeting
Jou Sun
and the eager expression of gratitude
everywhere I went
M'goi Sai

A piece of me remained behind
in Lam Tin squatter camp
and another in Tao fishing village
off Lamma Island - Hong Kong.

The other day I got a postcard
from Boundary Street
and another from Kowloon -
Their common message:
We are back to mainland China!
Reading between the lines
I offered a prayer accordingly
while in my mind's eye
an hour's Jetfoil cruise on the South China Sea
took me to Macao where
meeting Dr. Catarina Mok
we philosophically agreed, that whether Asian
African,
American or European,
the basic human values remain the same
and that the incarceration of Wang Dan
is a caging of every lover of freedom

The ghost of Tienanmen Square
shall be exorcised from all the four corners
of the world;
and from Africa and Zambia
I pledge my solidarity.

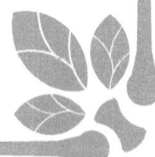

From birth to date

A fisherman by tribe
I smell fish in every situation.
Caution was part of my initiation;
I believe nothing of what I hear
and only half of what I see.
I have been cheated before
even by men and women of the cloth;
this world is full of deception -
There's an outbreak of human chameleons
and clowns
one needs an extra dose of caution

My journey began
on the shores of the big lake,
Bangweulu, July of Sixty
I wasn't born in hospital
they did not want me to be a Yes man
so a little hut in my mother's village,
freshly smeared with mud, served the purpose.
I was hilariously received by
elderly mothers of the clan
and a goat met its death at my birth
the village ate and rightfully drank
to welcome back a returning warrior
for birth then unlike now
was a blessing and not a curse.
A few days later
at the break of dawn
my umbilical cord got buried
in a simple but important ceremony
behind my hut of birth

linking me symbolically
to my people for ever
in life and death.
And so I grew up in the village
learning important lessons;
that honesty pays
dishonesty doesn't
and elders are elders
even if they be idiotic at times.
I learnt the power of dance
the beauty of song
the sweetness of communal fishing
and the curse of drinking or eating alone
I became a child of the tribe
with many mothers and fathers
and brothers and sisters.

But later
beckoned by neon lights
I left the village as was the fashion then,
I left the moonlight
the fresh waters
the folk tales and their simple lessons,
abandoning without conscious intent
the sacredness of the forest
in pursuit of enlightened ways
on city highways.
I graduated from the simple village industry
of tilling the land digging for roots,
catching small birds for food
I cast aside the fisherman's hook and net and canoe,
the rat-trap and all
I surrendered to the dustbin of so-called civilisation
to embrace a life of cinema
electricity and recycled water

a life of commercial treachery
technical misery
and social debauchery.

I am talking of days of subtle brain-washing
under the guise of education
salvation
liberation
emancipation.

I am talking of long months and years
of studying foreign people's victories
and my own people's 'follies'
sampling this "ism" and that "ism"
becoming in the process
a victim of dialectics
without a synthesis!
Then I slaved in factories
for illiterate industrialists
whose only "degree" was skin colour
and later for a deaf government
that would listen to no trade union
in the name of market forces.

I became a victim
of a callous system
rewarding dishonesty
and urinating on sincerity.

Recalling home
like the Prodigal Son
I suffered double vision
and for a while became a professional
schizophrenic.

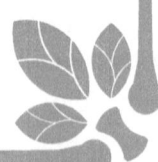

I got disgusted and protested
becoming a poet in the process
and grew a beard!

I still protest, and even tomorrow I will
still protest, marry a poetess and bear
more poets and poetesses so the world can see
Like I have seen
that it is a sin
for society to subsist
on the refuse bins of a few individuals.

I will lift a spear and enlist
with the ranks of those that fight with the heart
to set free
caged pigeons of peace.

At evening time
I will consort with those
that meet under the moon
to dance their sorrow and worry away

At midnight
I will seek solitude and find inspiration
through meditation
for a new formula
for the African rediscovery

In the morning
I will rise with the sun and endeavour
to give this amoeba world
a more solid shape

In the afternoon
I will plan with the brothers and sisters

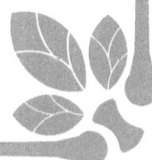

another dance for the evening
to remember all who have died of malnutrition
in a world where others die of indigestion,
I am planning a fitting
memorial service

Then the second night
I will offer an annoyed prayer to God
asking him where
in the present crisis He stands

And at the start of the next day
as if in the book of Genesis
I will start a recreation
to put the present set up
Up Side Down
level the field and sow the contagious wind
of justice

I am speaking of a rebirth;
I am talking of beating a new path
from this nonsense
to somewhere -
a departure from inertia
and the Mafia
to sanity and prosperity.
I am talking of a real
revolution of body
spirit and soul!
A re-Africanisation
of a people that won't be at sea
in the contrived
perilous ocean of globalisation.

Trouble with Government

If His Excellency, the President
doesn't preside with excellence
or the Honourable Mr. Speaker doesn't speak
with honour
and the august National Assembly
doesn't assemble with gusto
in the name of the People -
mwana -a storm is fast gathering
and a rupture is in the offing
the system is squeaking
the engine is smoking
the bun in the oven is burning!

And the oracle,
annoyed at the inertia in the nation
bemoans the abundance of political fodder
shoved down the throats of the gullible proletariat
who in turn keep themselves busy
fighting over the same trash
like flies over shit while political charlatans and
self-styled political engineers
graph one by-election after another
which they in turn win with the dexterity of
a clever chameleon
as it relishes licking one hapless insect
after another.

And then at night under cover of darkness
macabre birds sombrely congregate
on the village peripheral to mock the men folk
for letting themselves be turned into
political eunuchs

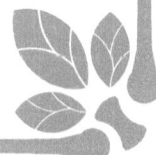

while the king and his cronies
enjoy a political diet
that makes them feast on the womenfolk
in front of the children.
Subsequently, chapel towers repeatedly echo in protest
one ancient hymn people love to so much ignore:
When will we ever learn
When will we ever learn!!??

The Struggle is the same, *mudala:*

For the fisherman frantically
struggling to keep the stubborn flies away
from his scanty catch

The sex worker desperately
soliciting
the non-enjoyable but inevitable services
of the next customer

Or indeed the trade unionist
trying to catch the attention of
a deaf government
the struggle is the same
the plight a common one
the fears and tears alike.

For the unemployed
facing an empty tomorrow

A mouse stranded in an empty barn
or indeed a nation smitten by
hunger and HIV/AIDS
the struggle is the same
the fears and tears alike
and a solution begs to be found
now now!

Still Black

I constantly yearn
for a naked bath
in the virgin river of unclothed truth

A bask in the tropical sun
of unwrinkled justice

I desire
a day-long romp on the sand
along the pristine beaches
of long unglorified
savannah lakes and rivers

I seek authenticity
between the creative thighs of
the great African heritage

In this self-bleaching
presumed dark continent
I remain by an act of
personal resolve:
a very Black Man.

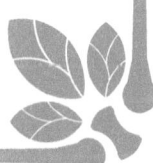

Lamentation of the heart

Who understands the anger
of a flower
whose pollen from the stamen
a bee without permission
has just taken?

Who can imagine the hurt
in the heart of
a raped woman?

Does anyone know
a farmer's sorrow
whose last seed
the drought has just gobbled?

Can anyone imagine the pain
in the fragile heart of a maiden
as she sorrowfully watches
her marriage chances
hopelessly lessen?

Does anyone fathom
the fury of a hen
whose ten chicks the hawk
one after the other
has mercilessly clawed?

Who understands the anguish
that fills the cold, long nights of a divorcee
or the loneliness of a pigeon
whose companion

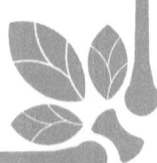

a village boy's catapult has just robbed
of its life?

Who comprehends
the undercurrents
in the anguished heart of a widow(er)
or the pains that silently eats away
at the heart of an orphan?

Does anyone know
the betrayal a poor fish feels
after believing with its gills
that the bait on the hook
was no fluke
but a gift?

Or indeed
who understands
God's own sorrow
when man lives without rules
his values sunken to an all-time low,
below zero?

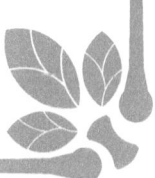

The traveller that I am

I cherish the *Cervecia*
and terrific Samba nights
of Campos do Jordao
the captivating sensuality of Rio de Janeiro,
Brazil,
accept my sentiments from across
The Atlantic Ocean
Mucho Gratia, Obrigado.

Botswana,
the sturdy ragged desert vegetation of the Kgalagadi
and the hospitality of your people
remain fresh in my mind
Dumela, Pula!

Malawi,
I vividly recall the weeping face of M'lanje
giving life to forests of tea and sugar
plantations below,
I miss the serenity and generosity
of the fisherman in Mangoche
Dzikomo Ndithu

Azania, South Africa,
the wonderful dance of resistance *Toyi-toyi*
was part of the victory miracle
only you can't resist forever -
learn to move forward as a nation

East Africa
Asante sana for your spirit of *Karibu*

I enjoyed the *pombe* and *nyama coma*
I contemplate permanent residence
may be in Kisumu or Mombasa

Europe - east and west
I remain fascinated
by your industrial stride
but learn to appreciate
life is not just about profit

Senegal,
the fishy stench of the sea
or the gory images of Goree island aside
what I had was a spunky time
someday I would return
as I miss *Le Grand Gazelle!*

America their America,
I promise to one day knock on your door
and see just what it is that makes you
so big headed

And Zimbabwe,
Chimurenga!
The Rhodesian days are now over
it is time to move on
on the wheels of consensus
there is a future to build
and a painful past that must be healed.
I will return for a dose of
Zambezi.

As for my beloved Zambia,
the less said the better
But never say die!

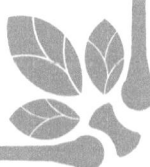

This Time Tomorrow

(An ode to African Writers)

Weep Not, Child
find solace in your own vow:
I Will Marry When I Want.
Cry, people of Azania, **The Beloved Country**
but this time with tears of joy and close behind you
the gates of Robben Island
as we Climb **The Anthills of the Savannah**
to commemorate with extreme pride
The Way We Lived before
Things Fell Apart!
Chant, without alcohol,
the sweet-bitter **Songs of Lawino and Ocol.**
And walk no longer in fear
Down Second Avenue or **Down River Road**.
March to the River Nile,
The Gambia and The Zambezi and bath
to kill the socio-political stench
of this pitiable continent.
Pick up the **Fragments** as you
weep for Johannesburg
mourn for Lagos and
cry for Nairobi and Lusaka.
Listen to the **Mine Boy** yearning for respite
protesting against total **Estrangement.**
In this new **Season Of Migration to the North**
must we still be
No Longer At Ease
in the mundane literary jungle
where reside the **Interpreters**

and **The Lion and the Jewel**?
Can't we as we explore fresh ideas
for Africa's real renaissance try
even for **A Few Nights And Days**
to dissect the complications
implications
imputations and insinuations of
Black and White in Love?
When we properly trace our **Roots**
we will discover every nation has its own
Okwonkwo
Kunta Kinte
Mathigari
and
Mandela -
A Man of The People.
And talking of people there are
People of the City
The Old Man And The Medal
The Concubine
A Woman In Her Prime
Houseboy
King Lazarus
The Poor Christ of Bomba
Chief The Honourable Minister
The Palm Wine Drinkard
Jagua Nana
The Minister's Daughter
Woman of My Uncle
or even the **Devil On The Cross!**
Must there still be any **River Between**
a people of common ancestry
or **Violence** indeed
when people can dialogue and reason?
Must there truly be any **Last Word**

as though **The Tongue Of The Dumb**
may not one day decide to debate its fate?
Meanwhile, mustn't we,
Because Of Women
who perpetually trudge **The Narrow Path**
revisit history so that
Facing Mount Kenya, or any black mountain
we all promise with Boy Scout honour:
I will Try and then embark on a new **Mission**
(not) **to Kala**
but from our cultural Diaspora to the old homestead
carrying in our hands
not **Petals of Blood**
but a romantic compendium of **Letters To Martha**
before we declare war solemnly:
One Man One Machete
no **Concubine**!
Aided by **The Barrel of A Pen**
we shall warn all in our way
Beware Soul Brother
as we proceed to prove wrong the claim
that **Africa Is Made Of Clay.**
Forgetting **The Sobbing Sounds**
of the OAU
we shall straighten out **The Crooked Rib**
and remind Africa of a new **Morning**
Yet On Creation day.
We shall talk of **Potent Ash** and remind everyone
There Are No Niggers Here!
We won't write about **Long Walk(s) To Freedom**
we shall brag about long walks in freedom
and **Write** not **What We Like**
but Like What We Write
proclaiming with benign contentment
Tomorrow Is Another Country.

The Beautiful Ones will have been born
and for those that love dance and song
there will be no **Cockroach Dance**
we shall proudly chant
Nkosi si Keleli Africa and
no one will wince in pain
or complain
What A Life
What A Husband
This Time Tomorrow
for **Africa** by then **Shall** truly **Be Free**
and we shall have learnt to
Lead like Madiba.

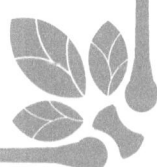

Laughter of an encounter

Memory can't erase
the healthy laughter of
our last encounter
as we lay on the sofa
myself listening
and you singing:
I will never find another you!

Since then
when awake
I am asleep
and in your arms
dreaming forbidden dreams!

Queen of the Namib desert
You are my love beacon in Windhoek
may the gods laugh with you
each time you recall
the laughter of our last encounter
Mwarerepo:
I will never find another you.

Tsunami in the city

I keep seeing the fearsome Tsunami
in the forlorn eyes of the citizens
(not residents) of Chibolya and Ng'ombe shantie
as they daily learn to manufacture hope
so as to successfully wad off
the fierce tides that sweep away in droves
those that lack the craft and clout
to successfully fight for survival
alongside rabid dogs and stray cats
on the choleric streets and garbage heaps
of the slum aggregate
some people dare call The City of Lusaka!

Hunger
disease
poverty - desperation
the story is the same countrywide
except at Parliament
Plot One
and OP[2]
where there are perpetual banquets
and the occupants only die of obesity and indigestion
while we die of chronic cholera
malnutrition and starvation.

Even the so-called National Budget
which ought to breathe fresh air into the
lungs of the economy

---

[2]   Office of the President (Intelligence Service)

is a Tsunami!
And the debris it leaves behind is a matter
for a sequel compendium
day after tomorrow.
Where indeed are we going if ever we are going?

Romantic letters of Yester-years

If only you and I
could piece back together,
those innumerable pieces of paper
upon which we in the yesteryears
scribbled with adolescent innocence, curiosity
and fervour
intimate messages of idealistic love
we later learnt
were actually beyond implementation
in real life.

With the benefit of hindsight however
they could just be
the tonic we all so desperately need today
to remind ourselves of the lofty heights
we once earnestly aspired to
in our romantic Olympic dreams.
They could perhaps serve as a yardstick
for starting things anew
and healing some of the bruises we have
sustained on the way.

Were it possible to retrace them all
those little pieces of paper carefully hidden
between exercise book pages
against the ever suspicious
teachers' eyes
and put them all in book-form
what a great book of love
that could be.

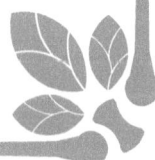

You see, I still recall
the depth and quality of our primary education then
and its rhythms and rhymes:
If all the lakes of the world were one lake
and all the trees of the world were one tree
and all the axes of the world were one axe
and all the people of the world were one person -

And if that one person were to take
that one axe and cut that one tree
and let it fall into that one lake -
what a great splash that could be!

Then we could probably carve that tree
into a new ark
and start life anew
closing the current
repugnant chapters of Sodom and Gomorra
which only occasion social diarrhoea
and political gonorrhoea!!!

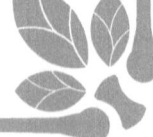

At least a line on the sands of time

As fierce flares fly wide and high
in the fireplace of my life
I panic
but quickly relax.

And as violent winds rekindle
stifled embers into flame again
I rise to the occasion
tuck my loin cloth
properly between my thighs
and squat on the ground
to write with my finger
the agony I have known
of a people living on leaves
their whole lives
as if they were caterpillars!
Of a people certain only of
uncertainty.

In my heart of hearts I swear:
The pens of poets
must never ever dry
and if need be
we must scribble with a finger
at least a line on the sands
of time.

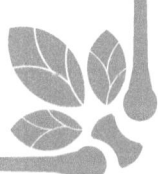

Letter to my Children

Hi guys, this letter is borne of
rare inspiration from a senior
African statesman Kenneth David Kaunda who,
also, once wrote a famous letter to his dear children.

As a child, I read that letter with fervour
and often wished my own dad had also written
one to me.

That, however, notwithstanding
my father made recompense
through frequent dialogue
which sometimes ended with a
generous dose of the stroke he, today claims,
was the needle through which
he injected discipline and integrity
into his beloved children.

The bottom-line though is to leave behind
a legacy for your children
so one day they never say:
We were never told!

Listen then, my children:
you come from somewhere
not from nowhere;
you come from a family
from a people and a tribe
from a nation and a race
you don't come from just everywhere.

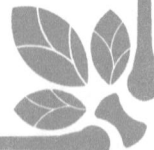

If you don't know yourself
you can't know others;
if you don't love yourself and your own
you can't care for others
and if indeed you can't manage yourself
how could you lead others?

Respect people
but never let them turn you into their
stepping stones;
refuse to be exploited.
I was long exploited on your behalf!

Demand your dues for an honest
day's work
don't slave like an elephant
and then live on an ant's diet
equity is a right we all must demand.

Remember to love your own children
at all times
it is only a fool that favours other people's
children at the expense of his own

And at the end of it all
have respect for elders,
seek God's face earnestly
and let him be Your Alpha
and Your Omega
for anything in between is
but a miasma that leads only
to eternal doom.
In my language we advise against
the philosophy of:
Ficili mwibala fya musha;

Ngafyapya ati, "We musha, selela uko,
Katoko kanoko"!*

[Editor's Note: *This means that the crops in a farm 'belong' to the slaves; when the crops are ready for harvesting, however, the owner of the farm takes full possession of the farm and chases away the slaves. In short, it's about how labour is not appreciated by those who own the means of production. Workers are just exploited for their labour without compensation.*]

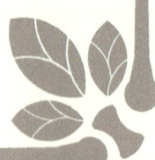

Woman, pearl of the nation

Eyebrow pencil in hand
I see you
sitting coquettishly before
your mirror
squinting your eyes and squashing your lips
all day long
in preparation for your night shifts.

I ask:
what work is this
you people do lying down?
Isn't a woman supposed to gracefully work
on her feet and not on her back?
And the treasures in your wardrobe -
an assortment of lipstick, wigs, artificial nails, nail polish,
eye-lashes,
perfumes, lotions to bleach your skin, lingerie,
tights, mini-skirts, and other skimpy clothing!
There can be no pride
in the women of a nation
working on their backs
dishing out sexual delicacies
even to strangers and children.

When the womenfolk lose direction
and begin to think through their lipstick
the nation chokes
and finally drowns
in its own social vomit and excrement.
A woman ought to be the pearl
not the curse of a nation!!

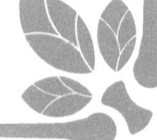

At the Master's word

I have toiled my whole life
and caught nothing;
it is at the master's word
that I keep casting my broken nets
over and over again,
and each time I decide
to cast my nets away and call it a day,
I hear by heavenly grace
the master's repeated command:
Cast thy nets into the deep!
And the toil starts all over again.
Meanwhile
my diminishing energy and weakening
will-power notwithstanding
I have come to know
the day isn't far
when my boat will want to sink
under a big, big catch
as the Lord honours his word,
mends my broken nets and turns me into
a real fisher of men!
I have come to believe in God
"Even though he is silent."

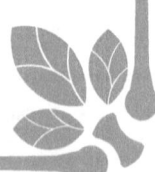

Political fodder

It doesn't matter
what they choose to call it

One party
Multiparty
Pro-party
Anti-party
No party
old deal
or new deal

If no food
no water
no job
no home
no school
nothing,
no past
no present
no future
what difference
does it make
what use does it have
it's all abuse
just another farce
sheer nonsense
It's the same mavericks
having a party
on behalf of the people
taking for a ride
as usual
the *hoi polloi* for an endless
merciless rough ride!

The Third Fight

Before we mop away
from the African floor
the blood of the colonial
debauchery
a more vicious battle ensues
from Monrovia
Freetown
Kampala
Kinshasa
Bujumbura
and Khartoum
We witness the arrival on the scene
of convoys of "new saviours"
emerging from the forests
comprising teenage forces
schooled only in ripping open
with bayonets and machetes
pregnant women
and nailing to the ground with bullets
those who dare ask
what is going on!
Tell the quartermaster
there is a shortage of mops
buckets and even water
to clean up the mess.
Then inform the people
a third fight is in the offing
to stop the second
and turn Africa around
hopefully for good
this time around.

The Refugee

One hasty step after another
in any direction except home
flight with no wings
from cold ashes of
a burnt down homestead
into the hollow world of uncertainty
fearful eyes red with panic
search for survival
anywhere
everywhere
except home.

So many lagoons to skirt
so many mountains and hills to
hastily climb and hurriedly descend
No compass to chart the route
no calendar to count the days
months or years
only the sharp sense of detachment
from familiar folks and environs
and a perpetual sense of loss
as one frantically seeks
a temporary, makeshift home
as a mere statistic in some refugee camp
anywhere, everywhere
except home!

And then after many,
many years of
anguish, sometimes
courtesy of the United Nations,
the refugee returns home,
to a home
that is no longer home.

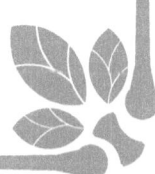

Sycophancy

Another name for
idiocy

Boot-licking -
synonym for lack of
personal identity

Loyalty -
polite word for stupidity!

And nationalism -
the name we all stupidly shun
without shame
not knowing it's the plasma
in the blood of a nation,
without which
we are simply cooked
stupid,
moribund and
dead!!

The oxygen
that defies all odds
beats pain
and makes us live
all over again!

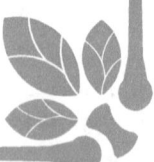

Pray for this world

people of God
pray for this world
think of the children
spare them a thought
do not rock their boat
these little harbingers
of future tranquillity,
do not abuse their innocence.

think of the women,
respect them
these custodians
of the vestiges of whatever
must have remained of
our now poor history,
do not squander the vitality
their simplicity,
respect their humility
they are God's most precious
gift to man.

and think of the poor
rob them not of life, their only treasure
do not let them perish from hunger.

look after the flowers,
wielding so much power in their petals
they brighten at no cost
the grey arena of life

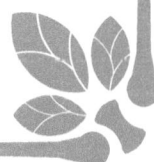

do not bleach their colours -
and spare a thought
for the invaluable treasure that is peace.

Every day, pray for this world
as you share God's word.

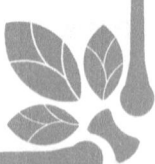

A Sad Song Indeed

Bosnia
Rwanda
Haiti
Burundi
Liberia
Somalia
Angola
Sri Lanka
Sudan
Pakistan!

A monotonous song indeed
A tune gone badly
as the UN drowns in its own tears
in spite of its long legs
as it tries to find its footing
on the slippery banks of
elusive peace
while those that await the calming down of the storm
wait only in vain
their desperate prayer for sanity always drowned
by machine gun fire!
But doesn't the UN know
who manufactures and sells
the Machine Gun?

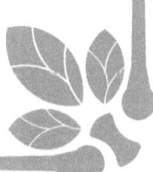

A Wretched Nation

Bottle after bottle
in a battle of no victories;
swig after swig
an entire nation including children
drowns into the fatal waters of
alcoholism,
while day after day,
hour after hour,
clad only in topless T-shirts,
miniskirts and high-heeled shoes,
teenage girls with livid morals
lose their virginity
on city pavements

And we all behave as though all was well
in the name of human rights and
individual freedoms, my foot!

Ngugi called them
Karendis of the easy thighs,
and Simoko, Golden Swines;
these girls of the disco generation
- even in Church, before the people of God,
they shamelessly sit
with their tempting legs wide apart
while their recalcitrant boys
liberally smoke *fwaka ya ci Ngoni (pot)*
and sniff glue non-stop
spending all their teenage years
in a perpetual stupor
from which they awaken only to retire unto their graves.

Isn't this a cultural mutation -
giving birth to a wretched nation?
And dying of old age at 20
as we now do,
we obviously can't be
progenitors of any future generation
There's no progression
no positive impression
only regression and decomposition,
concurrent dissipation of a people's total entity.
How can a proud nation hope to depend
for posterity,
on shrivelled scrota
of eighty-year olds
or indeed withered ova,
of women fifty and over
all because the younger generation has opted
to commit national *hara-kiri*!

We have shot ourselves in the foot
in this wretched nation -
aided by the HIV/AIDS pandemic.

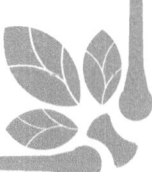

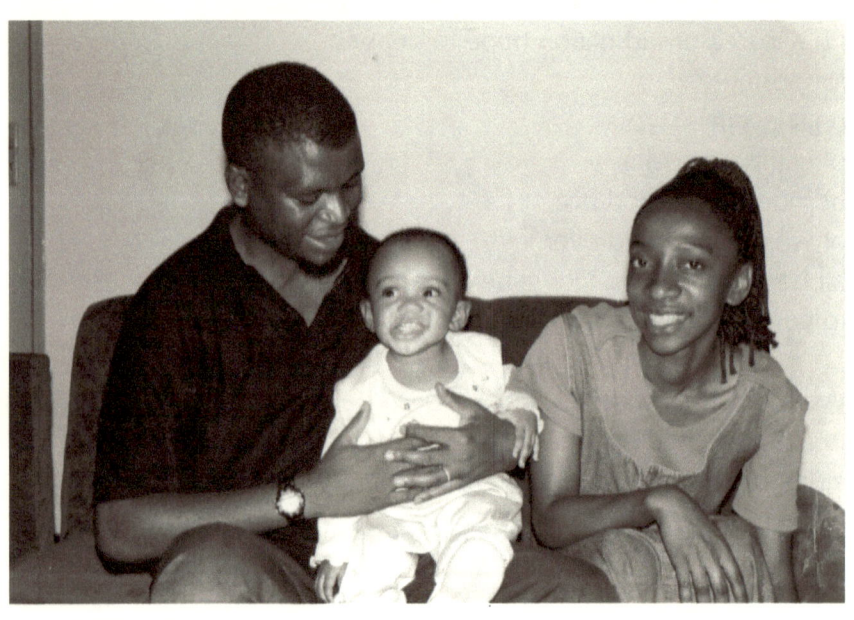

Mwange with daughter Bupe-Kunda and wife Katemba

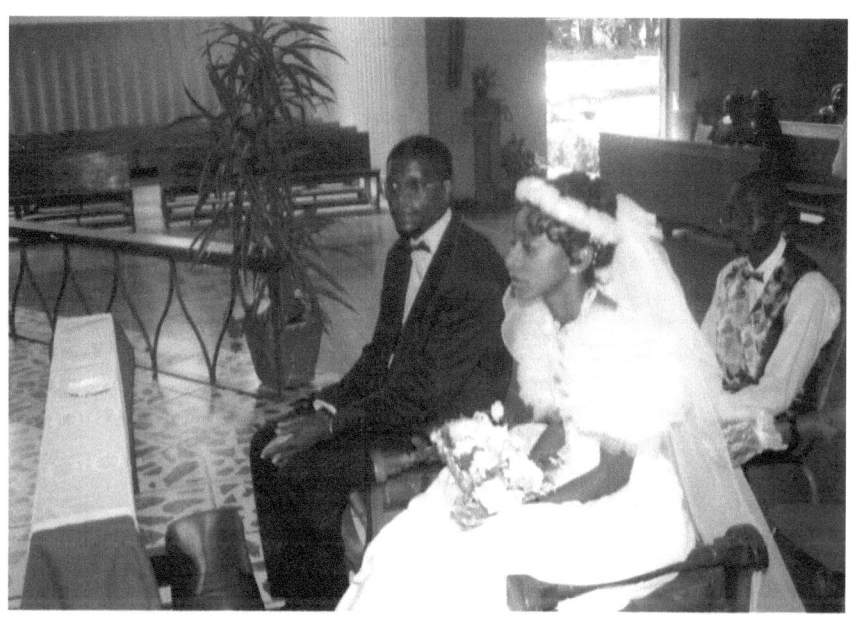

Wedding photo of Mwange and Katemba

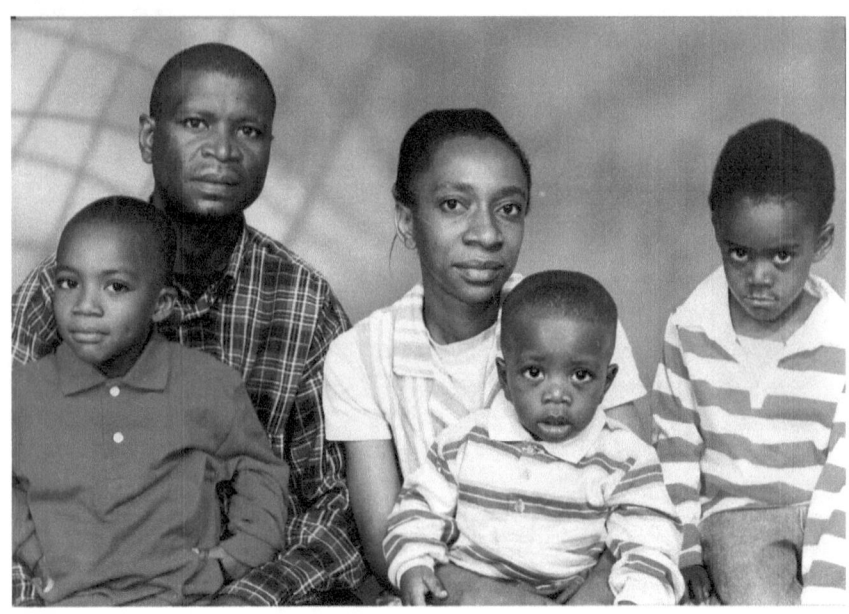

Family picture with the children; Mwange and wife, Katemba

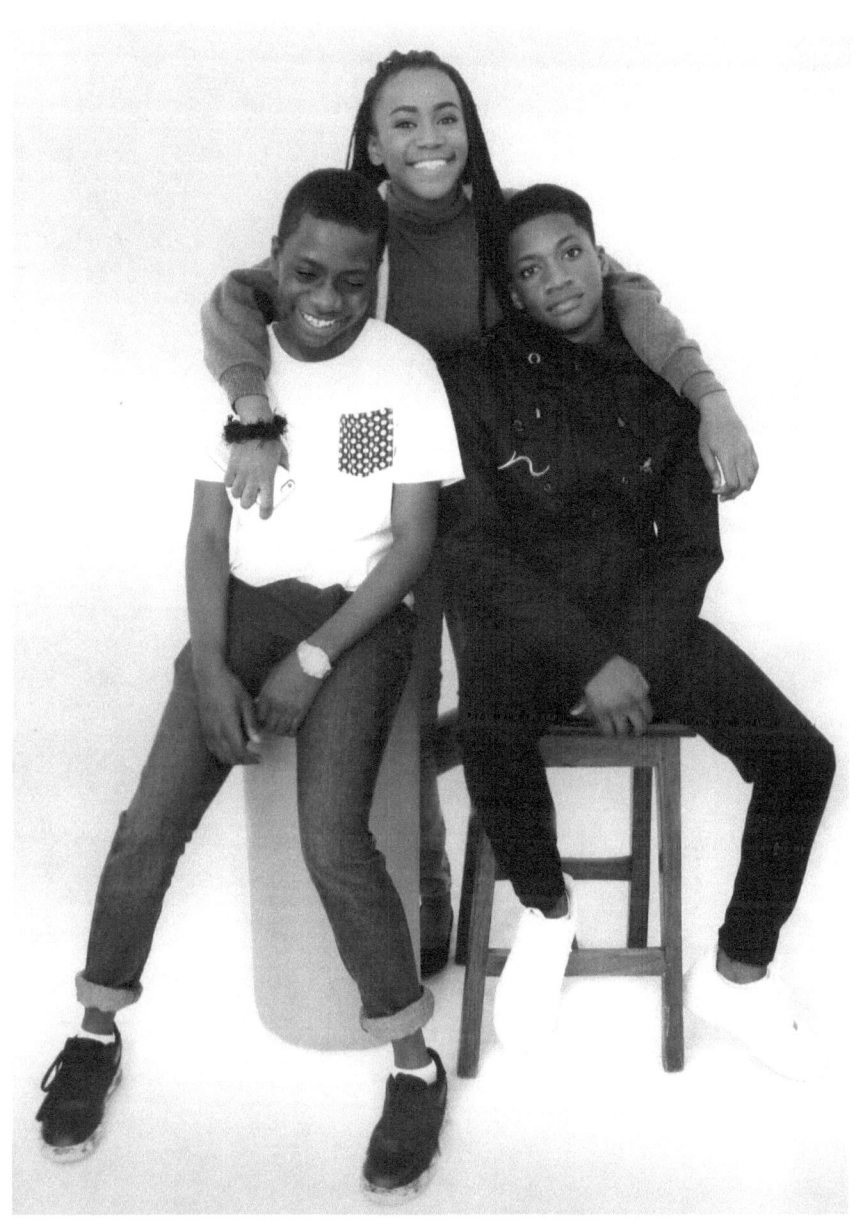

Mwange's children - Mwange, Bupe-Kunda and Bwalya

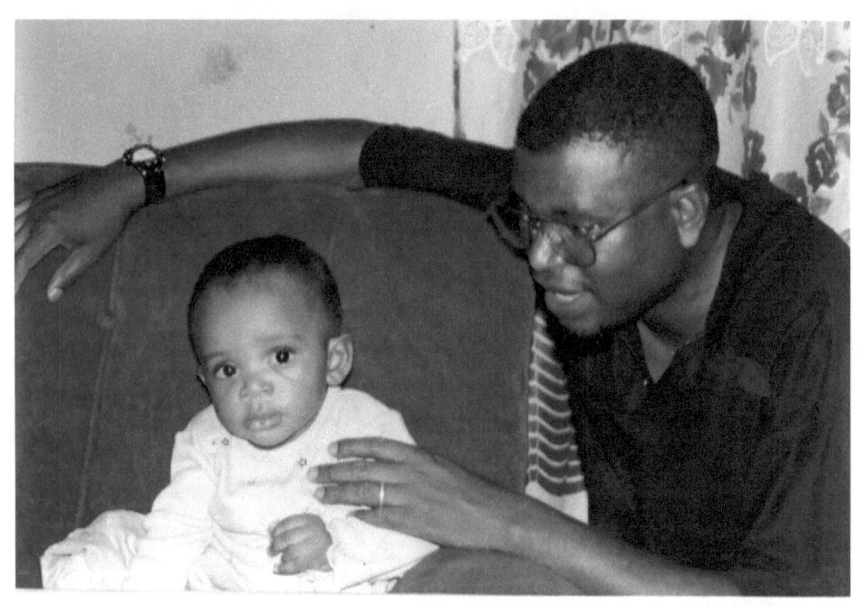

Mwange with his daughter, Bupe-Kunda Kauseni

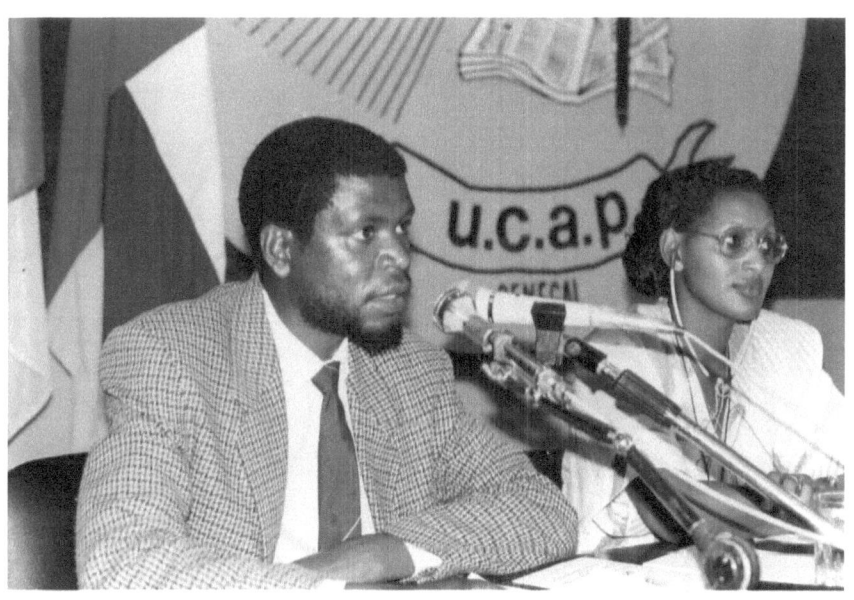

Mwange Kauseni making presentation at the meeting
for Catholic Journalists in Dakar, Senegal

About the Author

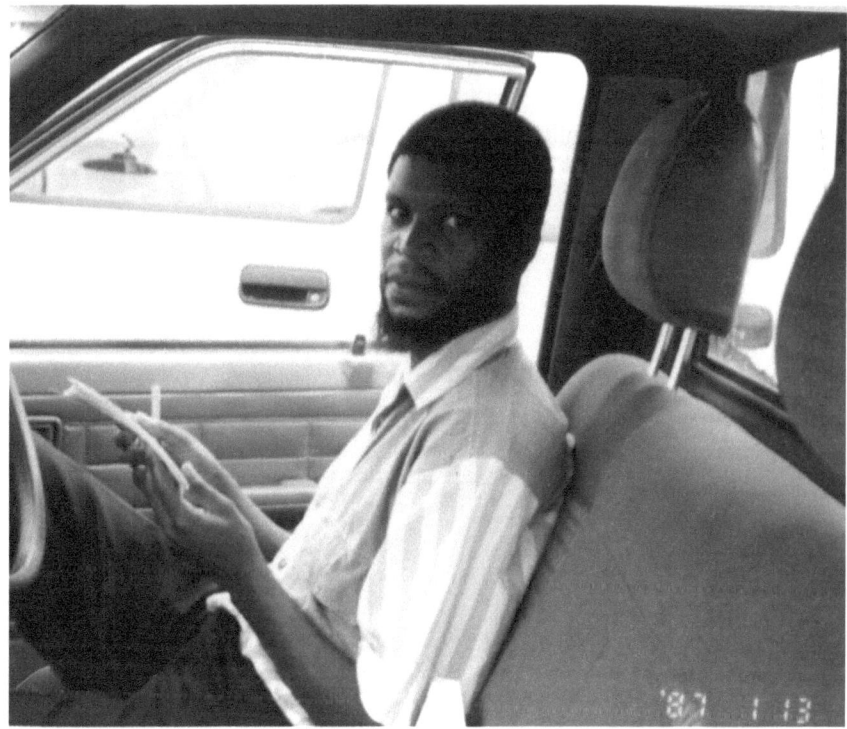

Mwange Kauseni was born in the Samfya District of Zambia in 1960, the son of a primary school teacher. He started formal schooling at Kasaba Mission and, in 1978, completed his secondary education at St. Clement's. His dream of becoming a Catholic priest was frustrated when, barely a few weeks before he was to be ordained a deacon in his fifth year of training, his superiors imposed an indefinite probation on him.

In 1982, not too daunted by the turn of events, Mwange became a class teacher at St. Charles Lwanga and Lubushi Junior Seminaries, respectively. He then pursued a journalistic path at Mindolo Ecumenical Foundation in Kitwe and set out to become one of the most distinguished and respected Zambian-born journalists of his generation. In recognition of his contribution to journalism in Africa, the International Network of Young Journalists (INYJ) conferred on Mwange the prestigious Journalist of the Year Award for Africa, in Geneva, Switzerland, in 1989.

Mwange worked both in his home country, Zambia, and Botswana as a features writer, editor, content designer, and media consultant. He traveled extensively around the globe.

Mwange died at the age of forty-six and is survived by his wife, Katemba, and three children.

www.ingramcontent.com/pod-product-compliance
Lightning Source LLC
Chambersburg PA
CBHW030908180526
45163CB00004B/1754